RUNAWAY
SLAVE
SYNDROME

RUNAWAY SLAVE SYNDROME

It's Not What You Think

Mitzie Holstein

MOUNTAIN ARBOR PRESS

MOUNTAIN ARBOR
PRESS *a Division of BookLogix*

Alpharetta, Georgia

ISBN: 978-1-6653-0729-1 - Paperback
eISBN: 978-1-6653-0730-7 - eBook

Printed in the United States of America

♾This paper meets the requirements of ANSI/NISO Z39.48-1992 (Permanence of Paper)

0 8 2 3 2 3

To the women and men of this world,
who struggle but refuse defeat.

Life will take us places,
but our destination is always ours to choose.

Contents

Author's Note	*xi*
Preface	*xiii*
Runaway Slave Syndrome: The Beginning	**1**
The Mind of a Slave	**7**
Tables Turn	**13**
From Church to Freedom	**19**
Return to January Sixth	**23**
It Got Dark	**27**

Author's Note

This book began in my heart.

It is written in the genre coined by me, "storytry" (storee-tree), which is a collection of stories told in the form of poetry. Every written word is from creative inspiration. Any similarities to characters, persons, or situations, are mere coincidences.

Preface

This book started as a story that began flowing as poetry, during a pandemic, when I thought that my creative juices were sapped. The events in the news, the reaction of the world, people, and places flooded into my mind; scenes from childhood became waves of emotions too. This created a canvas of what has become a book consisting of different stories—"storytry" (storee-tree)—stories written as poetry. It is intended to provoke, restore, and to explore perspectives by the many peoples of the world and for use in a college literature or gender studies course as part of an academic discourse.

Runaway Slave Syndrome: The Beginning

I was probably somewhere between the ages of ten to eleven years old when I decided that it was time to run away from home. Truth be told, I had (considering other homes) great parents, but I was still planning to run away. So, I began folding and keeping my "stuff" in one drawer in the dresser that my sisters and I shared. My mom did not find it strange when I later transferred those items to an old, empty *Dulcimina*, the Jamaican name for a particularly old-time suitcase. She just thought that I was being neat. To be honest, that *Dulcimina* was my getaway plan.

As a child, I was extremely precocious. I was never afraid to ask questions or place myself in vulnerable or dangerous situations, such as bathing in the river or treading unknown waters, crossing an extremely rough river during a huge torrent of rain, jumping from rocks into "strange" waters, playing hide-and-go-seek with friends, or being gone for long hours on various properties. While it was not unusual for such things to happen, being disobedient to a parent's warning to avoid such activities, or failure to complete chores, could land someone like me in "hot water."

So, at various interims, a beating from Dad would be in the making. Mom never spanked as often as Dad, but her beatings were solid and something to remember. But why was I planning to run away? Those beatings from Dad! Sometimes they were unplanned. For example, a neighbor might have told a story of seeing one of us somewhere, close to a bar, dance hall, a house we were forbidden to visit, or being in the presence of a boy, etc. This would bring on a whopping of undeserved proportions from Daddy. It was quite easy to see the emotions on his face as he entered the yard, and we would all scatter until he would loudly proclaim or call the name of the "guilty" party, which could be any of us. I never particularly liked to be hit; hence my decision to run away. That suitcase became my solace, as I folded, added, and made it clear to everyone to not touch my territory.

Now, everyone knows that to run away is quite a complex feat. Plans would have to go into play to make this happen. Being an avid reader, I remained with my books and planned and thought. *Where would I go? Who would I go to?* My dad was a seemingly important man, who, in my world, knew everyone. We lived in an area high in the Trelawny mountains called the "Cockpit Country." On one side was the mountain. Between the mountainside and our home were the streams, rivers, and acres of land, where all the catch crops, fruit trees, etc. were planted. The other side consisted of a narrow main road, low-cut hills, playfield (just up the road), and a bunch of other homes. In my mind, I was screwed. How could I run away without anyone seeing me? I had to then think of other obstacles to my plan, such as the gully below us that became filled up during rains, covering the banana trees located there, but would ultimately suck that water up with a huge gulp that could be heard by the neighborhood hours later. That place was unusually wet and murky most times, which would have been too much for me to handle as a child. The hills had pests and other unmentionables that would have been too dangerous for me as well. And what if someone caught and returned me back to my parents' home? My dad would kill me! So, I kept my ideas to myself. It was a plan that never went into effect, because the more I thought of it, the more dangerous it looked, and leaving my mother's cooking—not knowing whether or not I would starve—was probably too much for me to bear.

Now what does this have to do with RUNAWAY SLAVE SYNDROME? You see, I had planned and thought of all the consequences. This made me realize that I was better off living at home, in the safety of my parents, who, for the most part, were loving and caring in their own right. Slaves, on the other hand, made plans because they knew that being free was so much better for them than it was to live on a plantation, guided by the will of a "master," whose only plan was to overwork, underfeed, beat, molest, coerce, rape, and use until it was time to be discarded. Such slaves did not fear death or danger. They had already endured enough at the master's hand. Let's not forget that even a "loving" master had every potential to inflict bodily harm to his slaves—especially the disobedient ones. Sometimes it was done to pacify an enraged or jealous wife, who might have hated the attention he would give to a good-looking slave girl, or to adhere to "groupthink." He'd worry about how his peers would react to him not following the agreed-upon "rules."

Whenever a slave would plan an escape, a clear getaway was all he or she would have had in mind. The very idea of snakes, bears, insects, or bugs could possibly have seemed more intriguing than alarming, because he or she was already living under conditions of dire straits. With this out of the way, imagine a slave who had just made a successful escape from bloodhounds, bounty hunters, and beasts alike, and who would have found himself in a place of freedom. What thoughts would that individual possibly mull on? Now that the first goal has been accomplished, what would be next? Remember that there is already a bounty out for his capture. He would now have to mingle amongst this new population. Did he have his "free" papers? Even if he did, he would feel free to still think back on his wife, not wanting to be in her shoes. I am sure that, while plagued with guilt for leaving friends and family behind in the horror of their situation, this new freedom is something he would have wanted to keep.

Yet that could not prevent him from wondering and back-tracking to those small moments of "happy" times on the plantation, when he had hurriedly kissed and loved a woman, or cracked a joke about Massa to a pal. But would he ponder returning? I think not! For being on that plantation had not brought joy to his soul. At no point had he ever felt whole. Thus, his newfound freedom, no matter how small, would have been better than no freedom at all; knowing that back at the plantation he would only fall, and as a man, could never stand tall, if at any time he returned to the plantation at all, at all. Yet even this could not prevent him from having a "mindful visit" to the past now and then—Runaway Slave Syndrome.

The Mind of a Slave

While a slave who has escaped the plantation might revisit the past and pay attention to some of those meaningful times spent there with friends or family, he knows of the dangers, and would at no point have any plans to return. In that small window of time or escape, he would still watch with sadness, maybe hopelessness, but NEVER regret—unless it was him being sorry for leaving so many others behind. The kicker there, though, is that his escape would have caused tougher restrictions on those whom he had left behind, the murdering and/or torturing of close family members or friends; or even more thrilling, an escape proven to be a point of hope for those who would dare dream to do the same. For although Massa could beat and damage them for their actions and, sometimes, inaction, he did not have access to their rather prolific imaginations. He may have subjected their bodies to his will, but he did not have control of their spirits.

In the meantime, many slaves worked and hoped and dared to dream, and in their minds, they imagined themselves whipping their masters, living in the BIG HOUSE on the hill as "Miss Milly" worked diligently in the kitchen to do their bidding. For these reasons, they sang songs, cracked jokes, and laughed hard at times, because Massa could break their bodies, but not their imagination or will.

Such was the life of the slave: to survive, he did what he could; he knelt and prayed; for that, he understood, would keep Massa off his tail. He remained quite "good." Still, Massa could not see his mind or read his thoughts. For just as my obsession about running away from home had consumed me, so was he. His was a mind filled with fire, passion, rage. Often, he had murdered Massa in fits of rage, killed Massa's children, and fucked Massa's wife; but he still smiled, and chopped, and dug, head bowed low, saying, "Yes, Massa!" For you have not killed a man until you have broken his will to imagine, to think, or to consider himself to be as equal to the other, and yet to another man such as himself.

Now, this is not a scholarly report, or a thesis about race of any sort. It is about the ability of the mind I will proport; to see, imagine at its own will; after many had used countless tactics to quell the body and make it still. But a body that is not dead still contains a head—not brain-dead—that has a mind. That mind could run amuck or keep a man in a situation from which he would be unstuck. Yet it is that mind that would provide fortitude—a way of escape, not platitude—for slaves and their families, even after Massa's rape; for that "will," not even Massa could bind, gag, or tape.

What you don't understand, what you can't see, is that it is the MIND'S WILL that has kept Blacks living in these centuries. Do you think it has been about your laws, or Declaration of

Independence? 'Cause even with that, the BLACK CODES came; still, many cannot get in cadence; we straddle that very thin line of HOPE and DESPAIR; while in the mind of a slave, MASSA STILL DON'T CARE! The question now stands: where do we want to be? On this side, that side, or the side of HISTORY? History has its pits and its faults, I know, especially if the wrong ones tell the tale. How the minds perceive it will determine whether we'll PASS or FAIL. But a mind that seems broken at another man's will, even RUNAWAY SLAVE SYNDROME cannot dare fill. For the mind is a place where fresh ideas grow. No man or woman can make it corrode. It is the body that a man may break at will; but the mind's too far away—much too inaccessible for anyone's drill.

So, at this point, let's address the clatter. For too many, the "slave" does not matter. It is, after all, Massa who is in control; and it is from his switchboard that all matters unfold. Now, it can be difficult and cause much regret. This style of writing, some may not get. But it's the mind that has been on fire all this time. To dare to state what I now think may seem like a crime. Even while the body may be asleep, the mind is not necessarily at rest, as it courses the world's forests, savannas, and scenes, so prone to unrest. Out of the mind flows deep, dark thoughts; others so beautiful, creatively done, with such fervor, such passion, illuminated by the sun. You see, even in children, the mind still soars—active! Imaginative! At its best course. Even though with time, people seem to have lost their will, the imagination SPURTS forth. It cannot remain still. Now I beg to differ with those who think slaves were not SMART; if positions were switched, you would understand, deep from the heart, what it means to be enslaved or be free, and what it is to be on the right side of HISTORY.

It is indeed sad, but for now I must go—back to a place where I could function fast or slow. That's in the crevices of my mind, where ghosts would not dare tread, unless I give them room to browse or roam inside my head. I am at a place—a place where history meets my torrents or imaginative bursts and peaks. I burn with passion from within, and in that lies the mystery. From there comes my thoughts, hopes, and plans; ignited by something greater, divine, more amazing than myself. And in that fearless, hopeful space, is where I now can find the grace, to forgive and heal and grow. For in that space and in that time, no man can access what is mine. I HOLD it. I OWN it—a gift, a treasure trove, sparked in my imagination, given by God above! You see, it is He, who has given me life, and who has allowed me to be me. In all my aches and faults and sins, still gave me life, stirred from within—the ache, the agony; yet quelled the tyranny, fraught with such irony. He soothed the tears, passed down that ANCESTRAL TUBE; and showed me time and time again that He loves me, being part of His ancestry, tied to Runaway Slave Syndrome, the ULTIMATE MYSTERY.

Tables Turn

Have you ever left a place, a relationship, a job, or something else that once had an impact on your life? Most people can, in fact, identify with one or more of the ideas mentioned. When this happens, the Runaway Slave Syndrome can stretch its spider-like veins and corral an individual's mind into tunnels that form a never-ending maze—ones that set the mind ablaze. These tunnels traverse to places unheard; transcend dimensions too numberless, boundless from where many return broken, unbroken, or fierce.

Take, for example, a woman who has left a long-standing relationship. She was beaten, battered, bruised, and cursed, left for dead; still, she is "none the worse." Now, like a phoenix, she'll arise, standing tall, wings spread wide and free, telling stories to women like you and me, stories that transcend history. Her stories of days without bread, locked up in a room, passed out, left for dead. And in that moment, the story is told of just how much her spirit soared. The pain she felt, but still she knelt, and prayed to God for life, and a return to the path from which she had strayed. But her story does not end; for that woman, she does not bend. She rises again to fall in love with another kind of man, willing to take her in his cove. And once again, when garnered in, he crushes her hopes. She sinks within. This pattern undulating as sinuses drip with blood caused by another man's beating. And in its wake, a bellyache, aborted fetuses at every take. Still, she rises from the ashes, as days, months, and years she passes. Her life, a story that must be told. Her voice, a trumpet to be heard quite loud. Her sisters and friends call her "the little tramp"; from deep within, she knows she is not a scamp. They never knew about the rape, the times men covered her mouth with duct tape. To hide the shame, she took the loss, swallowed her pride, and pretended to scoff. Too many years already passed and gone; hardened she's been—still nobody's queen.

The death of one child, then another, could have broken this selfless mother. But she prodded on in silence, her friend, her passion, absolute resilience, her only presence. And in her mind, she continues to feel the passion, strength that grows as layers peel, and as she allows herself to heal; pulling back, each and every layer, reveling in harshness that has become pleasure. Now her stories inspire even women who can now retire. Such a woman has paved the way for women everywhere, who must then learn how to play, within the spaces of the mind, to which most do not understand how to confide. She inspires them to stand tall and proud. She allows them to do it both soft and loud. For the infrastructure of one's mind is very dear and one-of-a-kind, which even for a runaway, will feed and clothe her many a day.

Now, for that man, who has felt the pain, let down by a

woman yet again, who might have used him for his money to some degree, and has left him—a divorce decree. Oh dear! Oh dear! What will be the irony? It is the man who's now been hurt. A woman has stomped on his ego like dirt. He did not swell her eyes or punch her in the nose. He boiled water, took care of her feet and toes; 'cause he loved her—her head, her hands, her feet. He truly loves her, but now is in the heat.

So far, she has slept with his younger brother, his father, and closest friend; yet he stroked her head and still gave her bread. He moved away, cut all family ties. This love he has will linger until he dies. Yet she finds him, and once again, her charms, her ways, give him solace. Not once has he ever refrained from her embrace. The children, five and six, say, "Daddy! Daddy!" doing so many tricks. And he smiles, but within his heart, knows too well; the "prick" can't part, strikes him—a dart from hell. So, on that night in February, his soul got very fiery; as once again he caught her in bed with that man, who through the backdoor fled. "Uh, uh, uh . . . he's my brother!" she then said. Now he stands above her lifeless head, blood dripping, children screaming as he walked away.

His body was later found hanging from a tree. While two young lives, after witnessing this misery, must now grow up motherless—another one down in history. "He was a good man, an honest guy, a quiet man," some would utter. "Much too quiet," said another. "Bwoy like dem a serious brother!" Now here on this side of history, one page closed; yet opens another, to two children, without mother or father, trapped within the confines of, yet again, the Runaway Slave Syndrome.

From Church to Freedom

Today marked the day when her freedom papers came in. She looked at the envelope, and her heart skipped a beat. Her body suddenly became hot, sweaty. Confusion twirled; her gait unsteady, she had to get off her feet. She was not certain of what they had decided, but had made up her mind: in the church, she no longer confided. So, she slit open that envelope, and sure enough, there it was! ". . . So sad to see you go . . . You can return . . ." Blah! Blah! Blah! And in that moment, she became convicted; the decision to withdraw membership no longer afflicted. It did not matter what they thought, or whether or not she had fought and fought; whether to fast forward or to rewind, her decision was definitely not one-of-a-kind. People kept leaving the church, day after day. Still, she was unique—had done it her own way.

She had withdrawn her membership with a letter that had cut through all their BULLSHIT. It was time. She had had enough of biting her tongue—being shunned after seeing all kinds of stuff. Many could not take it. She was too much off-the-cuff. She thought of the times when she got a prophetic word, then thought of moments when she was seen but not heard. She knew at that time that the Lord had brought her in. Many times, later, wanting to leave, deeply worrying that it was a sin. She did not want to disobey, so she kept on going anyway. Many not knowing, that slowly inside, every part of her being was dying. She was longing to escape that "animal farm," being fed milk, when meat was what she needed—tasty and warm. She never wanted grass, because it tickled her throat. She wanted truth. She was bright and bold. But her light, very slowly, had begun to dim. They would not listen, would not dare let her in. She numbed her pain and smiled all the time.

One day, it had become too much. She was totally out of touch. Away from the Master was how she felt, while on that "farm," a blow was dealt. Then COVID-19 came. It was a time of uncertainty, but she was quite certain—no longer blinded by that curtain—a veil cast over the eyes; no longer seeking favor or a very big prize. She took time to pray and some days to fast. She had to let it out, leave it all in the past.

This decision making had her in a very scary place. But she took a chance, not minding the disgrace. Even on the days when she could not pray or felt that she never had anything to say, she dug her heels in, motivated from within. She could not just go looking back. And in the moments that she did, when many did not have a clue, knew well enough, that she had just activated Runaway Slave Syndrome. Today she celebrated. Her spirit was quite elated, and down she sat on that wooden floor, between the bed and the open closet door, looking at that envelope once more, to welcome freedom!

Return to January Sixth

A s we continue to explore this journey of the Runaway Slave Syndrome, let's return to January 6 of the year 2021; but this time, instead of a bunch of mostly white folks being prodded by a white president, imagine them being mostly Black, motivated by a Black president. The stage has been set. It is clear that a rally of some sort has been planned. There is going to be a gathering of thousands of so-called Negroes on the "Plaza." In such an instance, barricades would have been put up; policing would have been "beefed" up, and the National Guard would have had a heavy presence in Washington, DC. They would not have just been on "standby," because those in power would have dedicated themselves behind the scenes to make safety a priority. Thus, the "Attack on Democracy" would not have happened.

However, as we go full frontal in this setting, let's bring our minds again to that day. The Capitol is filled with Blacks who have guns and other weapons. They are assaulting police officers and have breached the Capitol building. Would they have survived? That's the question to ponder, and in my Runaway Slave Syndrome mentality (I went back there), I can see bodies on the ground, dogs biting, people being mauled, screeches and screams, as "Black blood," pardon my French, is spilled on Capitol Hill. They would have been treated in rather scathing reports as mobs and rioters, and their deaths would have been seen as a consequence of their own actions—the choice of trying to "attack the United States of America."

Imagine the faces of the reporters, the conversations in homes, as families lounged in front of their televisions! Black bodies everywhere, with no one else shedding a tear. Blood-curdling screams, written off as memes; as people snuggle closer together, only for their own brother. No wonder, leaving time to ponder, "Do Black Lives Matter?" and as we live our lives in this so-called democracy, where everything else is a fantasy, while others live in poverty. Will this, our story, ever end, or will we work to truly mend the broken pieces that hurt to the core, let hate rule as others are pushed out the door? For three hours and more, the president waited to "score." But what was the point? Everything was out of joint. And just like Nero, he waited; fires blazing—for him, quite amazing. Could a Black president have done this, with so much gone amiss? Still seeking an extra term, as we all continue to battle this "germ"? God forbid! For his term would have been one in jail; dragged from the White House, without thought for bail, as onlookers watched and many would yell, "Good riddance, nigga! You are a total fail!"

Let's not forget this inconsistency, which began way back in slavery. Let's look back, and quite at will, 'cause Runaway Slave Syndrome will make us ill, but will force us to understand, the ills of this land—cause us to burn inside as we seek to understand, compel us to peer deep into each other's eyes, to recognize that we, the people, are the prize; and when one man gets hurt, in each of us a soul dies. We must be forced to enter into his shoes; for when he is in pain, we do not gain, but lose.

It Got Dark

It got dark. The earth stood still as Claudette listened to his words; words that gave a sudden migraine; words that gave instant brain drain. She was at a loss for words. And she knew she had to say something. But how could she recover from such a bite—a sting that looked quite trite from the outside, but was already red and oozing with pus from inside. Daniel had said it. She was no longer his fit. She had "aged out." His latest fling was the newest thing. And that he would be with her forever, while Claudette, never.

She felt the pain, the years of all his cheating reign. She had stuck with him through the "thick and thin." And now he'd decided to bring someone else into his heart and their home. Good thing the kids were away at college. She had wanted them to get enough knowledge. She watched the woman between her sheets, face screwed up, sitting back on scraggly buttocks and knees. And even in it, she had no shame. Her eyes sparkled wide, saying, "Sis, I won this game!"

And as Daniel continued to spout the dirty, grimy words from his mouth, shameless and fearless as could be, her heart cried out, "Cree! Cree! Cree!" But Daniel would not let her be as he threw her faults in her face, he forgot her strengths, gave her no grace. She fought back waterfalls of tears that welled up from all those years. The memories rushed back in smiles and laughter; their only daughter, born from a teenage pregnancy, but from love, so amazing! How could this be? A son, spitting image of his dad—such a pity! Oh, so sad!

In her mind, she did contend that nothing could stop them.

They would always mend. The forgiveness given over the years had finally paid off. He had cried those tears. She thought his promises he would have kept, but she was WRONG, oh, boy! She certainly was. And in this moment, she understood. Daniel had to go; he definitely should. But this time, she would NEVER take him back. Oh no! She was going to get on the right track.

Such were the thoughts in her head, until she saw him on the floor—lifeless, dead! Her shoe heel had hooked him square in the forehead! Screams came from his new woman. She no longer had courage. As Claudette lunged at her, she cried with such might: "Please, please, I will make it right!" Shoe's heel in hand, Claudette held tight into her neck as she gurgled in fright. Eyes wide open, blood on the floor, her plight, her plight.

That girl killed was forever no more as Claudette straightened her wig, washed bloody hands at the sink, and walked out the front door. She was headed for the police station. She had settled the score. For years a slave to Daniel—no more! No more!

About the Author

Mitzie Holstein is a poet at heart. It is her goal to use her words to inspire and heal. Her messages are prophetic, inspiring, and touch the lives of those who read them. She credits her success to the Holy Spirit, her eternal muse. Mitzie has experienced the transformative presence of God in her life since March 2015. She has had many struggles in the process, but continues to look to God, who is her only source of comfort. Mitzie currently resides in Macon, Georgia, where she looks for inspiration around every corner.

Other Books
by Mitzie Holstein

Creative Streams: A Poet's Musings
Prophetic Moments and Prayers
Discovering, Hearing, and Understanding the Voice of God
Heart and Soul in the City
Knots in My Hair
Hands: A Book of Ten Poems

More Party Talk

More Party Talk

Answers to Everyday Legal Questions for Texas Lawyers

AUSTIN 2016

The State Bar of Texas, through its TexasBarBooks Department, publishes practice books prepared and edited by knowledgeable authors to give practicing lawyers as much assistance as possible. The competence of the authors ensures outstanding professional products, but, of course, neither the State Bar of Texas, the editors, nor the authors make either express or implied warranties in regard to their use. Each lawyer must depend on his or her own knowledge of the law and expertise in the use or modification of these materials.

The use of the masculine gender in parts of this book is purely for literary convenience and should, of course, be understood to include the feminine gender as well.

It is not the policy of the State Bar of Texas to assert political positions. It is our hope that this publication fosters healthy discussion about legal issues and the legal profession. Any views expressed in this publication are those of the author and do not necessarily reflect the opinions of the leadership or staff of the Bar.

International Standard Book Number: 978-1-938873-45-4
Library of Congress Control Number: 2016956365

Printed in the United States of America

Party Talk Contributors

Ramona Kantack Alcantara

Mark Andrews

Jacob Blizzard

John G. Browning

Suzanne Bryant

Bree Buchanan

William J. Chriss

Paul Coggins

David H. Donaldson, Jr.

Daniel D. Horowitz, III

Alicia G. Key

David C. Kroll

Mary A. Martin

Mike Maslanka

Mandi L. Matlock

Karen D. McCloud

Kim M. Munsinger

Carly Gallagher Murray

Robert Painter

Jack B. Peacock, Jr.

Carla L. Sanchez-Adams

Grant Scheiner

Christina A. Schuler

Jonathan Smaby

Briana Stone

C. Barrett Thomas

Natalie L. Webb

TexasBarBooks would like to thank the contributors who made this publication possible. For more information about the authors, see **http://texasbarbooks.net/books/more-party-talk/**.

STATE BAR OF TEXAS

2016–2017

Frank Stevenson, *President*

Joe Escobedo, Jr., *Chair of the Board*

Hon. Xavier Rodriguez, *Chair, Committee on Continuing Legal Education*

Joe Indelicato, *Chair, Professional Development Subcommittee*

Michelle Hunter, *Executive Director*

Contents

Preface   xi

Debt & Collections Issues   3

Criminal Issues   13

Employment Issues   29

Estate Planning & Probate Issues   37

Family Law Issues   45

Immigration Issues   63

Insurance Issues   67

Real Estate Issues   73

Social Media & Computer Issues   81

Miscellaneous Issues   89

Preface

Part of any professional's life is mastering the tools of the trade. Surgeons have scalpels, dentists have drills, and plumbers have pipe wrenches. Without these tools – and the training to properly use them – professionals simply cannot do their jobs.

But we lawyers? We don't really have highly-specialized tools that are unique to our profession. Our primary tool is our brain. Our jobs involve investigating, analyzing, organizing, negotiating, clarifying, articulating, and applying law to facts. Our ability to think and to know is at the heart of everything we do.

So unlike doctors and dentists – who don't carry their tools with them when they are "off the clock" – our brain is always with us. We can't conveniently leave it at home when we are out socializing as a way to avoid unwanted legal questions. Dentists are never asked to do a filling at a cocktail party, but our forays into the public sphere often involve strangers and acquaintances who use these chance encounters to pick our brains to get answers to their burning legal questions.

So to keep that brain as sharp as it can be, you'll need to have some passing familiarity with the most common legal questions the public might have. And once again, your colleagues are here to help. Like *Party Talk*, this book contains more expert answers to the questions posed to lawyers at parties, school events, and other public venues. Read this book, and you will once again be ready for whatever legal topic might come your way.

Of course, if you don't like answering legal questions from strangers, you can always skip the party and stay at home.

But you aren't going to do that, are you?

— Jonathan E. Smaby
Executive Director
Texas Center for Legal Ethics

More Party Talk

Debt & Collections Issues

How should I handle harassing calls from debt collectors?

Tell them the police will arrive to arrest them any minute if *they* don't wire *you* some money? Maybe tell them you sued them already and provide a made-up case number? Tell them you are a special agent with the secret Federal Department of Debt Forgiveness and you already forgave your own debt? Why not? The suggested responses are about on par with what you can expect from many debt collectors. The Federal Trade Commission reports complaints against debt collectors rose to the number one spot on its 2015 list of consumer complaint categories. Complaints against debt collectors made up 29 percent of all consumer complaints, more than double the number for the second-ranking category.

But let's review your options, seriously.

Debt collectors have the right to contact you by phone, letter, e-mail, or even text, as long as they disclose they are a debt collector and don't otherwise violate the law, BUT ONLY UNTIL you tell them in writing to stop contacting you. After that (and you will want to keep a copy of your letter, with proof you mailed it), a debt collector has the right to contact you only one more time to tell you what specific action they plan to take or to tell you they will stop contacting you (yes, I know. Silly, but true). You have the right to insist they stop contacting you even if you owe the debt!

The law requires debt collectors to treat debtors with respect, honesty, and professionalism. The Federal Fair Debt Collection Practices Act and the Texas Debt Collection Act protect debtors from the oppressive, harassing, or deceptive communications and tactics of debt collectors and creditors, including—

- telephone calls at work if the debtor has told the collection agency (or it has some other reason to know) the debtor's employer does not permit such calls;
- anonymous calls;
- repeated or continuous calls;
- obscene, profane, or otherwise disrespectful or abusive language;
- threats of violence, criminal acts, or actions the debt collector has no right to take; and
- deceptive attempts to discover personal information about the debtor or his finances.

Learn more about the protections available to debtors by visiting the website of the attorney general of Texas (**texasattorneygeneral.gov**), the Federal Trade Commission (**ftc.gov**), or the Consumer Financial Protection Bureau (**CFPB.gov**).

— Mandi L. Matlock, Austin

I discovered someone opened up a credit card account in my name and ran up a lot of debt. Do I have to pay for it?

The short answer is no, but it is going to take a lot of hard work to fix the issue and many different laws apply. Under each law, you must dispute the account within a specific time frame. It's always best to keep a copy of your dispute letter and send each letter by certified mail, return receipt requested.

Did you discover the account by looking at your credit report? If so, under the Fair Credit Reporting Act, you have the right to dispute the account to each of the consumer reporting agencies that list the account. Dispute the account *in writing*, include any supporting documentation (like a police report or an identity theft affidavit), and send it within thirty days of getting your report. The reporting agency must then conduct an investigation and notify you of the results within thirty days of receipt of your dispute. The way it conducts an investigation is by contacting the credit card company and asking for verification of the account. This is why it's a good idea to also send a copy of the dispute letter directly to the credit card company. If, after the investigation, the reporting agency concludes that the account does not belong to you, it must delete the information on the reports. If the account is confirmed to be yours by the credit card company, the reporting agency will leave the account on your report, but the account must be listed as "in dispute" and you have the right to include a 100-word statement about why you dispute the account. You can also request a block of the information, or you can request fraud alert or a security freeze to prevent future theft. You should consult a consumer lawyer for more information or if your dispute is not favorably resolved.

Did you discover the account by receiving a bill or statement? If so, under the Fair Credit Billing Act, you have the right to dispute the unauthorized use of the account. The dispute must be *in writing*, and you must send it within sixty days of receiving the first bill or statement. The letter must be sent to the address listed under "billing inquiries" in your statement. Once the dispute has been received by the credit card company, it must acknowledge receipt of your dispute within thirty days. The credit card company must complete its investigation before the end of ninety days of receipt of your dispute. Also, after receiving your dispute and before concluding its investigation, the credit card company cannot report the disputed account as delinquent to a consumer reporting agency, though it can report it as "in dispute." After the credit card company has concluded its investigation, it will either remove the unauthorized charges or conclude that you still owe the debt. If this is the case, you still have other legal remedies, but you should consult a consumer lawyer.

Did you discover the account by receiving debt collection calls or letters? If so, under the Fair Debt Collection Practices Act, you have the right to dispute the account. You must dispute the account *in writing* within thirty days of receipt of the first collection notice. On receipt of the notice, the debt collector must cease collection of the debt until it obtains verification of the debt or a copy of a judgment, or the name and address of the original creditor, and a copy of such verification or judgment, or name and address of the original creditor, is mailed to you. Again, it may conclude that you still owe the money on the account. If this happens, you still have other legal remedies, but you should consult a consumer lawyer.

— Carla L. Sanchez-Adams, Austin

You must dispute the account in writing.

I am thinking of filing a personal bankruptcy; what factors should I consider?

There are several factors to consider, but the initial threshold consideration is what you are trying to accomplish with a bankruptcy. A common misconception among consumer debtors is that once they file they can stop paying their mortgage, rent, or other ongoing obligations. That is false. Filing bankruptcy helps deal with past debts, but all debtors must continue to pay new bills as they come due. If your ongoing expenses are greater than your income, then, unfortunately bankruptcy may not fix that.

Title 11 of the United States Code, the Bankruptcy Code, provides a number of different options for a debtor to seek relief. While Chapter 11 cases predominate the news when it comes to bankruptcy, the primary forms of consumers bankruptcy are generally Chapter 7 or Chapter 13. A Chapter 7 case is considered a "straight liquidation" because it requires no payments; a trustee simply gets appointed to seize "nonexempt" assets and liquidate those assets for creditors. In all cases, you will have an opportunity to list some of your assets as "exempt," and the trustee will have an opportunity to object to your exemptions. You should visit with a consumer bankruptcy lawyer to advise you on your exemption options. Here in Texas, homesteads are generally exempt, except against the IRS, mortgage lenders, and mechanic's lien holders (like a roofer, painter, or contractor). Other assets that are exempt in Texas include one car per licensed driver in a family; jewelry up to $15,000 per couple; and certain types of life insurance policies.

On the other hand, a Chapter 13 case requires the debtor to commit to a payment plan over three to five years. You may be thinking: Why would I commit to a payment plan when a Chapter 7 is quick and easy? First, if you are behind on your mortgage or car payments, a Chapter 13 plan may be the only way to catch up on those missed payments. Second, Congress has amended the Bankruptcy Code to force more consumers into Chapter 13 payment plans instead of Chapter 7 liquidations. You should speak with a consumer bankruptcy lawyer about your bankruptcy eligibility and discuss whether a Chapter 7 is truly in your best interests, given the value of your assets.

Another very important threshold question you should ask is whether your debts are the kind that can be wiped out in bankruptcy. While many types of debts can be eliminated, not all debts are created equal. Debts owed to pay child support, taxes, student loans, and some others, generally speaking, cannot be wiped out in bankruptcy. Likewise, debts or judgments resulting from fraudulent behavior, such as embezzlement or receipt of fraudulent transfers, may be excepted from the bankruptcy discharge. Going through the process of bankruptcy is not free and, in some more complex cases, can be rather expensive. If there is risk that some of your debts fall into one or more of these "nondischargeable" categories, you should know those risks before filing and have a contingency plan.

— Mark Andrews, Dallas

While many types of debts can be eliminated, not all debts are created equal.

Criminal
Issues

The FBI shows up at your office with just a few questions for you. What to do?

Follow the Ten Commandments of Cooperation:

1. Don't panic. (Stay calm and go to the Second Commandment.)

2. Hire someone who knows what he is doing. (Hire a lawyer who understands the criminal process before talking to the agents.)

3. Determine your status in the investigation. (Are you a target, subject, or witness? The lawyer's job is to prevent today's witness from becoming tomorrow's target.)

4. Determine whether to cooperate. (If you bear little risk of becoming more than a witness, you may decide to cooperate.)

5. Negotiate ground rules for cooperation. (If you decide to cooperate, schedule the interview for a time, place, and duration convenient for you. If appropriate, bargain for immunity.)

6. Preserve all documents. (On notice of an ongoing investigation, preserve all documents or risk facing obstruction of justice charges.)

7. Preserve all privileges. (Never share your story with anyone outside the privilege without your counsel's blessing.)

8. Be patient. (You don't control the timing of an investigation. Accept it.)

9. Tell your story at the last prudent moment. (Taking an unprepared client to an interview gambles with his freedom. Before the interview, a lawyer must test his client's memory against documents and the recollections of others.)

10. Sell your story to the government at the height of the market. (The earlier in an investigation a witness proffers his testimony, the greater its value. Undue delay may diminish his value to the feds.)

— Paul Coggins, Dallas

Can a police officer order me out of my car?

Yes, a police officer may order you out of your car, in order to carry out any lawful purpose related to your stop, as well as to protect the safety of the officer or any other person. One of the most common, lawful purposes related to your stop is to search your vehicle—provided you give the officer either verbal or written permission to search or the officer has probable cause to search. An officer will have probable cause to search if he spots in plain view contraband (such as drugs or weapons) or if the officer smells marijuana. However, even if an officer does not have legal justification to order you out of your car, you should comply with the officer's request, but at the same time you may let the officer clearly know that you do not consent to the officer's actions. Once you have done so, your rights will usually be preserved and your lawyer may challenge the police officer's actions in court. Never argue with, threaten, or physically resist a police officer on the side of the road or anywhere else.

— *Grant Scheiner, Houston*

I am a licensed professional and was arrested; what do I do next?

Contact an attorney who handles licensing matters. Your local bar association can give you names of attorneys who practice in this area of law. Then you MUST self-report to your governing body (e.g., Texas Medical Board/Texas Board of Nursing/State Bar of Texas) as quickly as possible.

— *Mary A. Martin, Houston*

What are my rights during a "no refusal weekend"?

There's really no such thing as no refusal. A motorist always has the right to refuse to answer police questions, participate in standardized field sobriety tests (such as following a pen with your eyes, walking nine steps heel-to-toe on a real or imaginary line and walking nine steps back, or standing on one leg for thirty seconds with your arms at your sides), or voluntarily submit to the taking of a breath or blood specimen. A so-called "no refusal weekend" or "no refusal holiday" is typically when a local district attorney arranges for one or more prosecutors on twenty-four-hour duty to draft blood search warrants when motorists refuse to voluntarily submit to breath or blood tests. A judge is usually available on twenty-four-hour stand-by, in order to review and sign the blood search warrants, thereby speeding up the normal process for obtaining warrants. Once the police have a valid search warrant to draw a motorist's blood, the motorist may not refuse and the police may take the blood, by force, if necessary.

— *Grant Scheiner, Houston*

I was called into work and really need to go or I could lose my job. Do my children have to be a certain age before I can leave them home alone?

Texas law is not specific about what age is old enough for a child to stay at home alone. However, adequate supervision is the standard, and the adult caregiver is responsible for the child's care. Hence, inadequate supervision can be a kind of neglect. Texas DFPS recommends taking the child's age, emotional maturity and capability, disability status, and ability to respond to an emergency into consideration.

Under the Texas Penal Code "abandon" means to leave a child in any place without providing reasonable and necessary care for the child, under circumstances under which no reasonable, similarly situated adult would leave a child of that age and ability. The Texas Penal Code makes it a felony to intentionally abandon a child under the age of fifteen in any place under circumstances that expose the child to unreasonable risk of harm. The exception to that rule is the newest portion of the law that allows a child to be delivered to a designated emergency infant care provider which includes providers such as EMS or a hospital.

Inadequate supervision can be a kind of neglect.

— *Mary A. Martin, Houston*

Can I talk on my cell phone in a school zone as long as I'm using a "hands-free" method?

Ever looked in the lane next to you and seen that lady who is talking 90 miles an hour with her cell phone to her ear while putting on her makeup? Or, maybe you have driven next to the man who is talking on the phone and playing with his radio while drinking his morning coffee. There is no limit to the number of distractions people will take on while driving. The National Safety Council reports that 1.6 million crashes each year are caused by cell phone use while driving, and nearly 330,000 injuries annually are attributable to texting while driving. One out of every four car accidents in the United States is caused by texting and driving. Those are staggering and scary numbers. That's why in 2013 the legislature strengthened laws related to using a phone in a school zone or on school property. Texas Traffic Code sections 545.425 and 545.4252 outlaw the use of wireless communication devices while operating a motor vehicle within a school crossing zone, or on school property, unless the vehicle is stopped or the wireless communication device is used with a hands-free device. A "hands-free device" means speakerphone capability or a telephone attachment or other piece of equipment, regardless of whether permanently installed in the motor vehicle, that allows use of the wireless communication device without use of either of the operator's hands. All that being said, yes, you can use your cell phone with a hands-free device while in a school zone. Yet, a better bet would be not to drive distracted at all, particularly when a child's health or safety is at risk.

— C. Barrett Thomas, Waco

How long can a police officer detain me?
(For instance, do I have to wait while they
call a drug-sniffing dog?)

Under *Rodriguez v. United States* (2015), the Supreme Court held that a police officer may detain a motorist only for as long as necessary to carry out the purpose of the stop. For example, if an officer has stopped you for speeding, the officer may only detain you for as long as it takes to write you a speeding ticket or issue you a warning. Absent your agreeing to wait and giving the police verbal or written permission to search your vehicle, the police may not detain you in order to get a K-9 unit or a drug-sniffing dog, unless the officer has reasonable suspicion that your vehicle contains drugs or some type of contraband that a dog may recover. If you want to preserve your rights and challenge a police officer's actions in court, you should not answer any questions (other than to produce a valid driver's license, proof of insurance, and vehicle registration) and you should not give consent to the search of your person or vehicle. If the police order you to get out of your vehicle and to help facilitate a search by unlocking something, just tell the police officer, repeatedly, if necessary, that you do not consent to the officer's requests. Then comply and let your attorney challenge the police officer's actions in court. Never argue with, threaten, or physically resist a police officer on the side of the road or anywhere else. Most roadside police encounters are audio recorded and video recorded, so always be polite but firm in asserting your rights.

— Grant Scheiner, Houston

Can I legally carry a gun in my car?

Yes. Texas law allows you to carry long guns (rifles and shotguns) openly in your vehicle. For a handgun, you can carry a gun in your car without a license to carry if you are not a member of a street gang, are not committing an offense greater than a misdemeanor traffic offense* (e.g. speeding), and the handgun is not in plain view. If you have a license to carry a handgun you may carry it openly on your person if you have it in a belt holster or a shoulder holster. The gun may be loaded and fully functional in all of these circumstances. Technically, by federal law, you may not carry a handgun in your vehicle if you are within 1000 feet of a public or private school, although this is not frequently prosecuted. Also, if you have been convicted of a felony or an offense considered to be violence against a family member, you may never carry a gun in your car under any circumstances.

* A word of caution: if you are arrested for an offense like DWI or possession of marijuana and have a handgun with you, you will also be charged with unlawful carrying of a weapon because these are greater than class C misdemeanor traffic offenses.

— Jacob Blizzard, Abilene

Can I leave my child in my vehicle while I quickly run into the store?

The Texas Penal Code makes it a criminal offense to leave a child who is (1) younger than seven years of age and (2) not attended in the vehicle by someone who is fourteen years of age or older in a vehicle for more than five minutes. However, be aware that in Texas heat leaving a child of any age in a vehicle can lead to criminal prosecution for neglectful supervision or injury to a child.

— *Mary A. Martin, Houston*

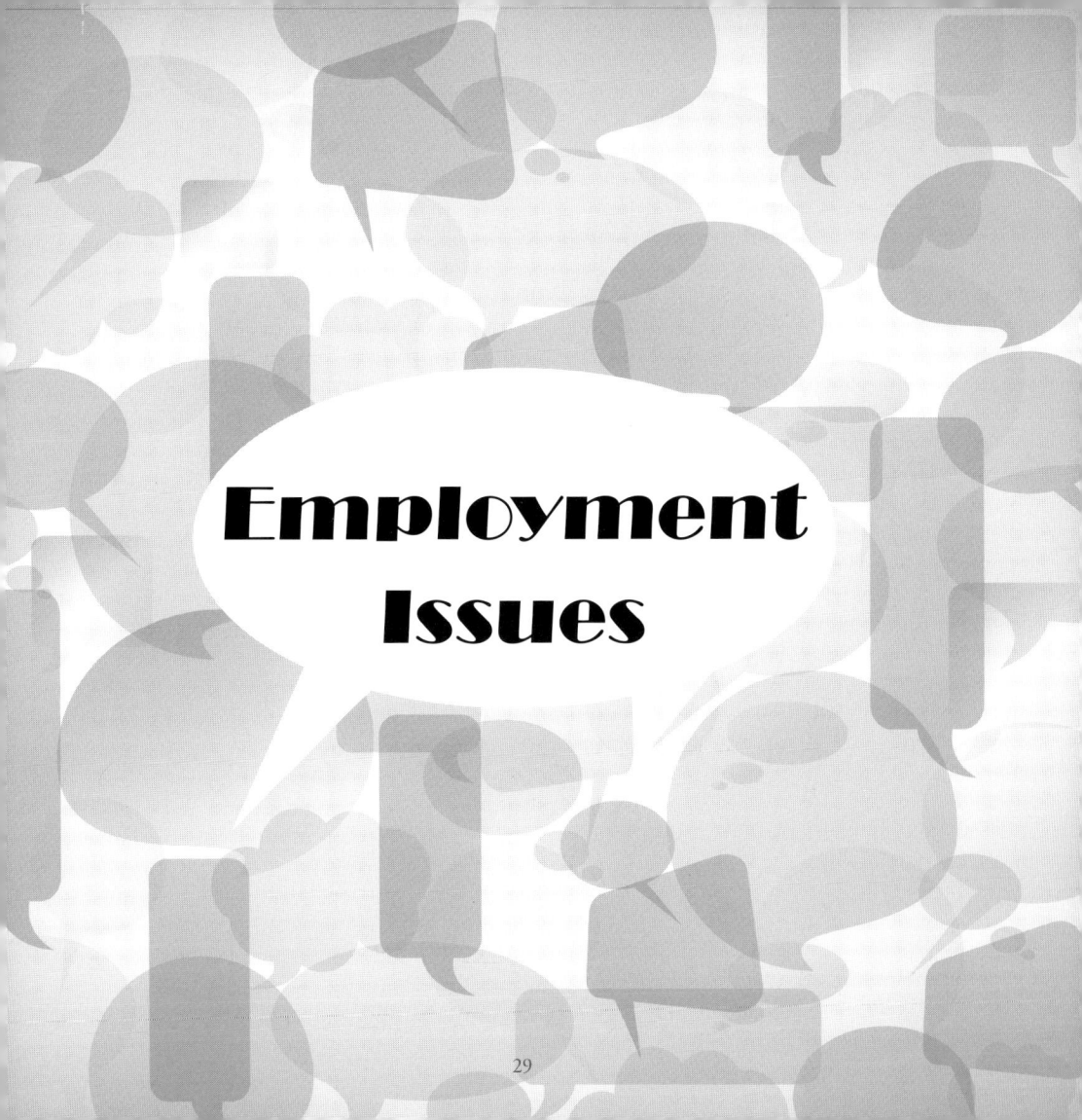

Employment Issues

Can an employer be liable for its employee's mistreatment of a customer?

That depends. Generally speaking, an employer is liable for the damages caused to a customer through the fault of an employee who is acting within the course and scope of his employment. But if the employee is not liable, then the employer would generally not be liable either. For example, if an employee faints without warning and through no fault of his own and then falls into and injures a customer, the employee would not be liable and neither would an employer unaware of the employee's propensity to fall because neither was negligent (at fault). While negligence is often the ground for imposing liability on the employee and thus the employer, it is not the only ground available. Premises liability cases (customer slip-and-falls) can be tricky and often require proof of more than mere negligence. And there are also varieties of intentional or willful torts, such as false arrest, that can create liability on an employee and, if he is acting in the course and scope of his employment, on the employer as well. Other types of intentional tort by an employee, such as assault and battery, may not result in liability on the employer because the employer will question whether the employee was acting within his job duties or rather attacked the customer as a result of personal animosity.

*— **William J. Chriss, Corpus Christi***

What does "at-will employment" mean?

We hear all the time about employment at-will. We often sign documents at work acknowledging we are at-will employees. But what does the phrase mean? What legal consequences flow from it?

Here goes: an at-will employee can leave work at any time and for any reason unless the employee has a contract of employment binding the employee to work for an employer for a certain period of time. By the same token, an employer can let an employee go for any reason whatsoever provided it is not an unlawful reason such as terminating an employee because of her race. Employers sometimes wave the magic wand of employment at-will way too broadly. One Houston court said that there was no at-will defense when an employer promised an employee that he would not be fired for bringing workplace safety concerns to management's attention. He did, he got fired, and a jury sided with the employee. The appeals court said that this promise was a binding contract that trumped the at-will doctrine.

— *Mike Maslanka, Dallas*

Employers sometimes wave the magic wand of employment at-will way too broadly.

What should I do if I am terminated and the employer asks me to sign a release in exchange for money?

Repeat after me: hit full stop! That's right; slam on the brakes. These releases mean that if you sign your name you give up any legal claim you might have against the employer. Forever. And employers have been known to sneak in a noncompete agreement in the release. Hire a lawyer for an hour or so to review the agreement. Trust me, you feel a lot better by considering your options. These agreements should ideally be looked at by a board-certified labor and employment lawyer. Look at it this way: What's the harm?

— Mike Maslanka, Dallas

What does "right to work" mean?

This is perhaps the most misunderstood phrase in employment law. "Texas is a right to work state and I can fire you if I want!" says the employer. Wrong! Here is the origin of the phrase. Employees have a right under the National Labor Relations Act to elect a union to represent them, including having the union enter into a contract on their behalf. Federal labor law leaves it up to the states whether to require the employees to join the union as part of the contract. Those states, like Texas, that refuse to allow this practice are called "right to work" states. That is, those employees are still represented by the union, but they need not join the union and become dues-paying members.

— *Mike Maslanka, Dallas*

Estate Planning & Probate Issues

What happens when you don't have a will?

If you die without a will ("dying intestate"), the laws of your state will determine who inherits your assets and how much each person will receive. These laws vary from state to state. Generally speaking, the distribution of your assets will be largely determined by whether you die married or single and by whether you or your spouse or partner has children. For example, if you die single with no children but your parents are alive, your parents will likely inherit under the state's plan; if your parents predeceased you, your siblings—if any—would likely inherit. In short, in the absence of a will, the state is trying to "second-guess" what you would have wanted to happen.

Of course, the state's choice of how to distribute your property may not be your preference at all. That's why it is critical to have a will and keep it up to date. Review your will after any major change in your life, such as marriage, divorce, moving to another state, or the births or deaths of family members or others you may wish to inherit from you.

— *David C. Kroll, Austin*

My parents are getting older.

What can I do to protect their assets?

Do mommy and daddy know you're asking? If your parents still have their wits about them, they need to be fully involved in this discussion.

If you just have general concerns about protecting assets, I'd suggest visiting an estate-planning attorney. An estate-planning attorney can provide disability documents to help manage assets while your parents are alive and wills or trusts to protect assets after they pass away. While an estate-planning attorney can help before disability arises, they are generally ineffective if the client doesn't know the natural objects of their bounty.

If your parents have lost the ability to make decisions for themselves, a guardianship might be an option. But, generally speaking, a guardianship is unnecessary unless there's fighting among the family about who should control the assets or a parent is a danger to themselves. A guardianship should not be your first option, as it's costly and it affects your parents' rights.

If Medicaid is in the foreseeable future, you need to run, not walk, to the nearest supplemental needs attorney. A good supplemental needs attorney knows the ins and outs of Medicaid and just might save your parents from accidentally disqualifying themselves.

There's no way to protect assets from every scenario but you sure won't be helpful if you don't even know where to find the assets. Work with your parents now to compile a complete list of their assets so you aren't fumbling around later searching for that random property in Montana they mentioned thirty years ago.

— *Christina A. Schuler, Houston*

Is there a way to leave my house to my kids without probate?

Absolutely. It all depends on how much you love your kids . . . or how much effort you're willing to expend.

There are various ways to keep your house out of probate, and some options are better than others.

The newest option is the statutorily blessed transfer on death deed (TOD), which allows you, as the owner, to designate beneficiaries on the deed while retaining full rights to the property. Bonus: it's revocable if your kids act up.

A ladybird deed allows you to designate beneficiaries while retaining full rights to the property, with the additional bonus of allowing your agent under your power of attorney to execute the deed. So, if you're slightly bonkers, you, or rather your agent, might want to run with this deed rather than the TOD. It's also revocable.

Another option is to name remainder beneficiaries on a life estate deed. You retain only a life estate in the home, which means that, while you can occupy and use the property during your lifetime, you cannot sell or give away the house without consent from your remaindermen.

You could opt to outright give your property to your kids through a gift deed, but you cut all ties to the house on execution of this deed.

A house may pass through a trust, but this requires quite a bit of preplanning and, generally speaking, is not a great option for most people.

The general rule is that deeds accelerate mortgages, invalidate insurance, and forfeit homestead property tax exemptions, so it's wise to talk to your insurance agent, mortgage company, and attorney before whipping up a new deed.

All in all, the simplest option for you is to do nothing and let your kids worry about the mess.

— Christina A. Schuler, Houston

Family Law
Issues

I don't want to spend a lot of money on my divorce; can my spouse and I use the same lawyer?

No. A divorce lawyer can't represent both parties. The problem is that the lawyer must be the advocate for his client, and the lawyer can't advocate for opposing parties. However, a lawyer can represent one member of a couple, and the other member can be unrepresented. The problem with this, as you can imagine, is that one member of a couple will have an advocate and the benefit of legal advice, and the other member won't. The outcome might be fair, but how would the unrepresented member even know without a lawyer?

— *Kim M. Munsinger, San Antonio*

Can my marriage be annulled?

As a divorce attorney, I hear a lot about whose fault it is that the marriage failed. She cheats. He spends too much money. We just don't love each other anymore. But with legal annulment of a marriage (as distinguished from annulment of a marriage through the church), the focus is not on the spouses' deeds or misdeeds after the wedding. Whether a marriage can be annulled will depend on premarital "deeds or misdeeds." Was one of the spouses underage or under the influence at the time of marriage? Was one of the spouses mentally incompetent or divorced less than thirty days? Was one of the spouses forced or otherwise defrauded into the marriage? If so, if something prevented one of the spouses from freely giving legal consent to be married, then the marriage may be able to be annulled. Once the marriage is annulled, it's like it never happened.

— *Carly Gallagher Murray, Austin*

After several years in a relationship, my lesbian partner and I decided to have a child with the help of a sperm bank. We intended to be equal parents. She gave birth to our baby, and we raised our daughter together for six years. Now, my partner has found a new love and moved out. She will not let me see my daughter. Can my partner just take my child from me? Would it have been different if we had gotten legally married?

Since you never adopted your daughter you are a nonparent, or legal stranger, to the child. You may end up not seeing her until she is an adult. Hopefully, you have not waited too long to take legal action and can establish standing so you can tell the judge your story. If you can establish standing, the next hurdle will be to overcome the parental presumption in Texas Family Code, which directs a judge to grant custody to a parent over a nonparent, if both parties are equally fit. Being married doesn't really matter since it creates a spousal relationship—not a parental relationship.

But don't give up hope. As judges begin to understand LGBT-headed families, there are more cases where the judge will consider the importance of the second parent's relationship with the child. Contact an attorney who is experienced in LGBT custody cases immediately—and encourage your friends who are LGBT parents to legally adopt their children.

— Suzanne Bryant, Austin

I have full custody of my sixteen-year-old son. Lately he has been staying at his mother's house without my approval. What can I do?

Dealing with teenagers can be challenging. And this particular legal issue is one of the most challenging in the family law arena. You might want to consider legal action to enforce your custody order *if* you believe your son's mother is encouraging him to stay at her house without your approval or if you're seriously concerned about his safety and welfare.

The legal action available to you is actually one against your son's mother. It's her obligation to facilitate his return to your home at the appropriate time, and she could be found in contempt of court if she is actively discouraging his return—and maybe even if she is passively failing to insist that he go. But if she can show he won't cooperate and she can't make him leave—a sixteen-year-old is even harder to drag kicking and screaming than a two-year-old—the court will probably deny your request to enforce the custody order by holding her in contempt.

If you do feel your son is in danger, you can ask the court to issue a writ of attachment, which would direct the sheriff to take custody of your son and deliver him to you. Because this is a rather drastic measure, the request must be accompanied by an affidavit clearly stating facts that demonstrate the action is necessary to protect your son.

The best case scenario would be to discuss with your son's mother an appropriate response to his behavior and agree to a custody arrangement going forward. You can agree to alter the custody and visitation schedule at any time and in any manner. If the two of you can work toward the common goal of achieving an amicable resolution and encouraging your son's cooperation, he will surely benefit.

— *Alicia G. Key, Austin*

A sixteen-year-old is even harder to drag kicking and screaming than a two-year-old.

Do I really need a lawyer to get a divorce?

You're not required by law to have a lawyer to get a divorce, but that doesn't mean you don't need a lawyer. Divorces are technical and can be complicated, and the information about them that is available on the Internet is often incorrect. Do-it-yourself divorces can lead to unfair outcomes and mistakes that need to be cleaned up later—if they can be—by hiring a lawyer. The best approach is to get lawyer referrals from people you trust, interview a couple of lawyers, and hire one to represent you in your divorce.

— Kim M. Munsinger, San Antonio

You're not required to have a lawyer, but that doesn't mean you don't need one.

I'm thinking about filing for divorce.

Should I delete my Facebook page?

No! Deleting evidence that could be relevant in a lawsuit is called spoliation of evidence. A party has a duty to preserve evidence when the party knows—or reasonably should know—that there's a substantial chance a claim will be filed and that evidence in its possession or control will be material and relevant to the claim. Therefore, if you are thinking about filing for divorce, you should not destroy or alter potentially relevant evidence—including social media accounts or their contents. A spoliation finding by a court could have serious consequences, including an award of attorney's fees or costs to the harmed party, exclusion of evidence, striking a party's pleadings, or even dismissing a party's claims.

If you are thinking about filing for divorce (or are in the middle of a divorce), you should be mindful about what you post on social media. There is nothing wrong with making accounts private before or during divorce proceedings, but even with private settings, anything on your page may be viewed by "friends" who may be connected with others with whom you didn't intend to share information. Although you should *never* delete any social media pages or contents during a divorce or in anticipation of divorce, you should consider "going dark" and stop posting to those accounts. Social media is an evidentiary gold mine in divorce proceedings—anything you post can (and probably will) be used against you!

— Natalie L. Webb, Dallas

Is legal separation a good idea?

There is no such thing as a legal separation in Texas. All property—including income, retirement funds, and the like—acquired during marriage is presumed to be community property unless proved otherwise by clear and convincing evidence. Even if you and your spouse decide to physically separate, community property continues to accumulate up until the date of divorce. Yes, you heard me correctly! In Texas, even after you file for divorce, the community estate continues to accumulate until the date the court signs the divorce decree or the parties sign a partition agreement. Why is this important? Because the community estate is subject to a "just and right" division between the parties on divorce.

If there are children involved, both parents have equal rights to possession of the child unless there is a court order that dictates the rights of each parent. If the parents are separated and the child primarily lives with one parent, there is nothing to stop the other parent from taking or keeping the child unless there is a court order in place. If the police are called, the responding officer will probably advise the calling party to contact an attorney, because the issue is a civil matter between spouses. If you are contemplating separation, it is a good idea to speak with an attorney to discuss your specific situation.

— *Natalie L. Webb, Dallas*

Why is it important for children in LGBT-headed households to have two legal parents and how can this be accomplished?

Thousands of Texas children who are being raised by same-sex parents are vulnerable because only one parent is a legal parent. A second-parent adoption creates two legal parents with equal rights and responsibilities. If the legal parent dies, the child is not an orphan, and there will not be a custody battle with the deceased parent's family. If the second parent dies, the child is eligible for survivorship benefits, e.g., Social Security or military. If the couple breaks up, the relationship between the child and both parents is preserved so the child will have the love and support of two people.

After gay marriage became the law of the land, the Texas Vital Statistics Unit began listing the birth mother's wife as the second mother on the child's birth certificate. While this certificate is an indication of parentage that might be accepted in a doctor's office, it is certainly not legal proof that will be accepted by governmental agencies or in court. The only certain way to establish a parent-child relationship is through adoption. An adoption order establishes a permanent parent-child relationship that will be honored by courts in Texas and other states.

— *Suzanne Bryant, Austin*

Last week a young man contacted my brother and said he is my brother's son. (His mother is an old girlfriend of my brother's.)

What should my brother do?

Remember the Russian proverb adopted by Ronald Reagan as his signature phrase? "Trust, but verify." If your brother wants to know for sure, the question can easily be answered with a DNA paternity test. This could be a very delicate issue, which your brother probably shouldn't broach with his potential new son on their first meeting, but I would definitely advise *my* brother to do the testing. Simple and inexpensive testing kits can be purchased online or at the drugstore, completed at home by rubbing a cotton swab on the inside of the cheek, and submitted to a lab for testing.

If it is true, do they want to establish a legal parent-child relationship? If so, what benefits and obligations would attach? That largely depends on the age of the "young man."

Assuming this alleged son is eighteen years old or over, only he can file an action to establish that relationship. There would be no particular obligations created by the legal relationship, but benefits, such as inheritance rights, would be established. If the kid is under eighteen, on the other hand, a court order establishing the parent-child relationship would create a whole range of rights and duties for your brother, including the duty to pay child support.

— Alicia G. Key, Austin

Immigration Issues

My fiancé is not an American citizen. Will he/she automatically become one once we get married?

No! Your spouse does not automatically derive U.S. citizenship through marriage. Immediate relatives of U.S. citizens do take priority in the hierarchy of family-based immigrant petitions. However, you will need to ask yourself a number of additional questions, including: "How did my spouse last enter the country and what is his or her status now?" "Am I an American citizen?" "Has my spouse ever been deported?" "Am I sure?" "Does my spouse have a criminal history?" Your answers to these questions will determine the amount of paperwork you must slog through before your spouse can become a lawful permanent resident and, eventually, a citizen. In any event, it's a good idea to consult an experienced immigration attorney to ensure that you complete the process correctly.

— Robert Painter, Austin

It's a good idea to consult an experienced immigration attorney to ensure that you complete the process correctly.

Insurance Issues

A customer at my bar had a drunk-driving accident after drinking too much at my establishment. Am I liable?

If the customer was provided an alcoholic beverage at the bar, the bar may be liable for the damages the drunk driver causes in a wreck. In order for the bar to be liable, it must have appeared to the server that the customer was obviously intoxicated to the extent that he presented a clear danger to himself and others at the time he was served the alcohol. However, the bar may be able to avoid liability based on the "safe harbor" defense. The safe harbor defense protects the bar owner from liability if the bar required its employees to attend a TABC approved seller training program and the server actually attended the training program.

If the plaintiff is able to show that, in the past, servers were directly or indirectly encouraged by their employer to violate the law regarding selling or providing alcoholic beverages to intoxicated persons, then the bar will not be protected by the "safe harbor" defense. It should also be pointed out that, since 2007, the courts have allowed juries to compare the responsibility of the bar alongside the responsibility of the drunk driver, which has greatly reduced the potential liability of the bar.

Last but not least, most commercial liability insurance policies specifically exclude coverage for liquor liability claims. If the bar wants the security of insurance protection, the bar must make sure their insurance contains a separate liquor liability endorsement.

— Daniel D. Horowitz, III, Houston

What are the parents responsible for if a teenager has an automobile accident?

Like many legal questions, the answer depends on the specific facts. The general rule is that parents are not personally liable for the negligent driving of a licensed teenager. However, the parents can possibly be held responsible based on a negligent entrustment theory. If the child is driving a car with the parents' permission and causes a wreck, the parents can possibly be sued for negligent entrustment. To be liable under this theory, the facts must show that the child was an incompetent, unlicensed, or reckless driver and the parents knew or should have known the child was an incompetent, unlicensed, or reckless driver.

In most situations, when the teenager gets in a wreck, the parents' auto insurance will cover the claim. However, more and more insurance companies are selling policies that provide coverage only for family members specifically listed on the policies. Parents should pay close attention to the insurance coverage they are purchasing to ensure their teenagers will be covered if they get into a wreck.

*— **Daniel D. Horowitz, III, Houston***

I loaned my car to my friend and she didn't have her own insurance and got into a wreck. Is the friend covered under my insurance since I wasn't in the car when the wreck happened?

There is no certain bright line answer to the question because it depends on the language of the policies involved and as to who is covered and the specific facts involved. Ask your agent for your policy. Look for specific language and definitions regarding who is a named driver and any endorsement that may exclude certain people. Most Texas policies also exclude coverage for racing events and intentional acts (e.g., road rage).

— *Mary A. Martin, Houston*

Real Estate Issues

My landlord filed bankruptcy. Am I going to be evicted?

So your landlord filed bankruptcy, and you are a little nervous. That's understandable. The good news is that it is pretty unlikely that you are going to be evicted. Why? One simple reason: unless you are not paying your rent, the landlord and his creditors are interested in keeping all of the tenants and collecting all the rent. After all, the landlord needs to collect money to pay back his creditors and evicting a paying tenant is not going to help him. But, suppose you say, the landlord may be able to raise the rent by kicking me out and replacing me with another tenant at a higher rate. What then? Unless the landlord has managed to find such a tenant who could move in right away, he will not risk the rent interruption. Second, the Bankruptcy Code provides a protection for tenants in section 365, which essentially protects you under the terms of the lease until it expires. So is there anything you should worry about? Yes there is. What about the deposit you left with the landlord when you signed the lease? You may want to see if he still has it in a separate account. If not, my advice is to get a lawyer!

— *Mark Andrews, Dallas*

Can my homeowners association make me pay the association fee?

Generally, yes. The ways in which the homeowners association can make you pay the fee vary depending on whether you are in a condominium or a noncondominium owner association. The terms in the governing documents for the owners association can also affect the ways in which the association can make you pay the association fees. These governing documents must be recorded in the real property records to be enforceable. They typically are called and include a "Declaration" for condominiums and "Covenants, Conditions & Restrictions" for noncondominium developments.

Unless the governing documents provide otherwise, (1) a condominium association has a lien on your property to secure the association fees, including any attorney's fees and other costs associated with collection if you do not voluntarily pay, and (2) you are personally liable for all these fees and costs. This means that the condominium association can foreclose on your property through a relatively simple nonjudicial foreclosure process and sell your property to recover what you should have paid. In addition, the condominium property association can sue you, obtain a judgment against you, and collect against your other personal assets.

A noncondominium owner association typically also has a lien but must file a lawsuit against you to foreclose on that lien. The noncondominium association is also more limited in its rights to foreclose. It cannot foreclose if the only amounts you owe are for fines or certain collection costs. The noncondominium association can also obtain a judgment against you and collect against your other personal assets.

If you do not pay and the association has not otherwise collected against you through foreclosure or lawsuit, you likely will have to pay the amount you owe (plus interest and possibly penalties) once you decide to sell or refinance your property. Title companies handling these transactions will pay to the association what you owe out of your sale or mortgage proceeds at the closing.

— *Ramona Kantack Alcantara, South Padre Island*

I just received a foreclosure notice from a lender I've never heard of. What should I do?

The first thing that I would do is contact that lender and try to find out what connection that it has, or claims to have, to my loan. Then, if I am not satisfied with their answers, I would retain counsel to file a lawsuit and ask for a temporary restraining order to stop the foreclosure. The only way to stop the foreclosure is to file for bankruptcy, but that would ruin your credit. If you don't stop the foreclosure, you could lose the title to your property.

— Jack B. Peacock, Jr., Dallas

If you don't stop the foreclosure, you could lose the title to your property.

Social Media & Computer Issues

Can I ethically store client documents

or information on the cloud?

Currently, twenty state bar associations have issued ethics opinions regarding cloud computing or cloud storage; unfortunately, Texas is not one of them. But in looking at these opinions, each of them has adopted a "reasonable care" standard for lawyers to follow when storing their clients' data or documents in the cloud. Common aspects of this "reasonable care" standard include understanding the basic concepts of cloud storage technology or consulting with an expert who does, taking steps to select a vendor who agrees to keep the information protected and confidential, and consulting with your client about its needs and thoughts regarding cloud security. Lawyers should be careful to distinguish between "public" cloud service providers (such as Google), which may waive responsibility and liability for data security, and "private" cloud providers (those not generally available to the public). Many legal observers have concluded that public clouds are not appropriate for a client's confidential information. In short, while use of cloud computing by law firms is widespread and ethically permissible, lawyers must still take steps to use such services in a way that provides a reasonable measure of security.

*— **John G. Browning, Dallas***

Do I need to post a disclaimer statement on Facebook in order to prevent all of my personal content from going public and being used without my permission?

It wouldn't be a bad idea, although you might also wish to protect your content through the use of available privacy settings. You see, while Facebook's own terms of service provide that "you own all of the content and information you post on Facebook," you agreed as a Facebook user to give the site a nonexclusive, worldwide free license to use any of your content—including any intellectual property like photos and videos. And when you publish content when your Facebook profile is set to "Public," Facebook's terms of service state that you are allowing everyone (including people off of Facebook) to access and use that information, as well as to associate it with you (i.e., your name and profile picture). Bottom line, the best way to protect your posts from being used without your permission is not through a disclaimer, but by limiting access to these posts in the first place through your privacy settings.

— John G. Browning, Dallas

Can I sue for defamation if someone posts an untrue statement about me on social media?

Sure, but it's complicated, and it had better be worth it. Putting a statement out on social media where others can see it is a "publication" just like a newsletter or a flyer. If the statement is one of fact (opinions and epithets like "Stupid is as stupid does" or "you got ugly all over you" or "you drive like a madman" don't normally qualify), then it needs to be something really bad and preferably cause serious financial damage to make it worth your (and your lawyer's) time.

Statements that are truly damaging to someone's business or reputation ("You defrauded me and fifteen other members of our church out of thousands" or "You were operating on my Dad while you were drunk and you killed him!" or "I know you are plotting a terror attack on Six Flags") can be defamation whether they are on Twitter, Facebook, or on the front page of the newspaper.

Be aware that Texas law protects comments by the willfully ignorant and stupid by requiring that, as the offended party, you must prove that the person making the false factual statement about you was negligent—he knew it was false when he said it or, using reasonable care, should have known it was false. And if you are a public official or a public figure, you pretty much have to prove they knowingly and intentionally lied about you.

Even so, anything short of truly devastating false factual statements on social media rarely call for a lawsuit given the exaggeration on social media and the way we tend to discount statements on it. And most false claims are better dealt with through more speech debunking the claim than a costly and debilitating lawsuit.

If you do have a good defamation claim, though, there are several hoops to jump through to actually file a suit and to recover damages—more hoops than normal for most other lawsuits.

Under Texas law, you have to give the person a chance to take it back and show that you did so before you bring a lawsuit (that's probably a good idea in any situation anyway). You should also be aware that if you don't have a good defamation lawsuit and you file suit anyway, Texas has a statute that allows the person you sued to try to recover his costs and attorney's fees from you.

So yes you can sue, but I wouldn't recommend it unless there are provably false facts that the person knew or should have known were false and there are serious, provable financial damages.

— David H. Donaldson, Jr., Austin

Miscellaneous Issues

Is the legal system rigged?

Well, let's see. The customary definition of a "rigged" system is one in which the outcome is fixed so that the winner or outcome is decided in advance. For the legal system to be rigged, the outcomes of hearings, trials, negotiations, mediations, etc., would have to be predetermined. For that to happen, lots of people would have to be in on it.

After all, there are many different players in our legal system. Typical lawsuits have at least two parties, at least two lawyers, and one judge. If the trial judge rules without regard to the law, it can be (and usually is) corrected by an appellate court of different judges. For that many people to get together to rig an outcome would be extraordinarily unlikely, to say the least.

That doesn't mean that inequities or crooked lawyers and judges don't exist. But lawyers are investigated and punished by the bar all the time for wrongdoing, and no one has trouble finding a lawyer to sue another lawyer. For every lawyer who does something corrupt, there are many more who are highly motivated to call attention to it.

Think about this: judges regularly rule against the government when it is party to a lawsuit, even though the judge may be dependent on *that same government for his regular paycheck*. It's so routine we don't even think about it. And if the government itself can't rig its own legal system, who can?

— *Jonathan Smaby, Austin*

How can I find a good lawyer in my area?

The best approach to finding a good lawyer is a personal referral. Therefore, ask your family, friends, and business associates. Ask them if they know any lawyers who can help you with your legal problem. Ask them what they know about the lawyer and what they think of the lawyer. In addition, if you know a lawyer, ask her for a referral to a lawyer who can help you with your legal problem. Lawyers know other lawyers. Therefore, although the bankruptcy lawyer you used two years ago may not handle divorce cases, she will likely know a lawyer who practices in that area.

Another option are lawyer referral services. Most local bar associations have programs through which it will refer you to an area lawyer for legal advice or representation. Most lawyer referral services screen the lawyer prior to listing him with the service. In addition, most lawyer referral services require the attorney to carry liability insurance. Also, most lawyer referral services provide an option for you to meet with the lawyer for a limited time for a small fee to discuss your legal matter and determine if you and the lawyer want to work together. Because lawyer referral services vary, ask how their lawyers are screened and what qualifications they are required to have to be included with the service.

The websites of local bar associations and specialty legal groups are another source for finding a good lawyer in your area. Many of these groups provide a directory of their members divided by practice area on their website.

If possible, try to get at least two referrals. Talk to each lawyer personally. Ask pertinent questions to determine the lawyer's knowledge of the law concerning the particular area of your problem. Ultimately, your goal is to determine whether the lawyer is someone you would be willing to work with over the next year.

Good luck!

*— **Karen D. McCloud, Dallas***

I'd like to do pro bono work but I don't know where to start.

A great way to get involved with pro bono is to visit the State Bar's pro bono website, **ProBonoTexas.org**.

There you can enter the type of pro bono opportunity you are looking for, and it will identify all the organizations that meet the criteria you selected. Once you find a pro bono opportunity that appeals to you, you can contact the organization through the website and sign up for a case or another type of volunteer work. There are also lots of tools and resources on Pro Bono Texas to help you with your case.

Another way to get started with pro bono is to contact your local legal aid provider directly and ask for the Pro Bono Coordinator. The Pro Bono Coordinator will be able to help match you with the case or other volunteer work that is right for you.

Don't forget to bring your friends! Many pro bono cases are great opportunities for teamwork. If taking on a case on your own seems intimidating, recruit a friend or colleague and tackle it together.

Finally, if you want to do pro bono, but you don't think you can take on a case yourself, be a mentor. You can sign up to mentor other attorneys in your practice area on Pro Bono Texas. You can earn up to five hours of CLE credit, including one hour of ethics for serving as a mentor or a mentee on a pro bono case.

*— **Briana Stone, Austin***

> Don't forget to bring your friends! Many pro bono cases are great opportunities for teamwork.

What should I do if I suspect a lawyer has a drinking/drug problem?

The best place to start is with a call to the Texas Lawyers Assistance Program at 1-800-343-8527. You will speak to a lawyer with specialized training in the identification and treatment of substance use disorders. Know that your conversation, as well as your identity and that of the person about whom you're concerned, is confidential by statute. In fact, if you prefer, you may call anonymously. TLAP will help develop a plan for reaching out to the lawyer, which may include crafting a way for you to have a conversation with her/him or for TLAP to make the call. Additionally, TLAP has over 850 trained volunteers across Texas who stand ready to reach out to and help impaired lawyers move towards recovery.

You should also take a look at rule 8.03 of the Disciplinary Rules of Professional Conduct, which mandates reporting to the disciplinary authority a lawyer who has violated one of the Rules that "raises a substantial question" as to fitness to practice. If, however, the lawyer suspects the other is "impaired by chemical dependency . . . or mental illness," he may report the other to TLAP instead. The identity of all involved will remain confidential. Additionally, compliance with any treatment suggestions is voluntary. The lawyer for whom you are concerned will not get into trouble if you call TLAP.

Aside from professional duties involved, know that your partner may be dealing with a substance use disorder that, by medical definition, is progressive and can be fatal if not treated. With treatment and a program of abstinence the chances for recovery are excellent. If you find yourself in this situation, please make the confidential call to TLAP and develop the plan that will best support you and your partner, as well as protect your firm and its clients. You can find resources and more information at **www.texasbar.com/tlap**.

— *Bree Buchanan, Austin*

What is an expunction, and can I get one?

Or, can I get my "record sealed"?

An order of expunction, if granted, is that your eligible criminal records are literally destroyed and cannot be seen by anyone. You are most likely eligible for an expunction if your case was dismissed or you were found "not guilty" of a criminal charge by a judge or jury. If you have other criminal history or were arrested for multiple offenses at one time, you may not be eligible for an expunction.

You must petition the court in the county of the offense requesting that the records be expunged. What actually happens is you choose all of those agencies and entities that you think have copies of criminal history related to the arrest and prosecution (e.g., the jail, the police department, DPS records division, and the FBI records division).

If you pled guilty or no contest in a court and were placed on deferred adjudication probation, then you are not eligible for an expunction, but may be eligible for an order of nondisclosure. An order of nondisclosure effectively seals your record from public view. After you complete your probation and the waiting period (five years for a felony), you can petition for the order of nondisclosure. If granted, an ordinary person or employer could not just look at your records, but government agencies, including police, and licensing agencies (e.g., Board of Nursing) can still see your record. Some offenses are not eligible for a nondisclosure because of the nature of the offense (e.g., any sexual-based offense).

— Jacob Blizzard, Abilene